THE LAST BLACK
MECCA : **Hip Hop**

A Black Cultural Awareness Phenomena and It's
Impact On The
African-American Community.

by

Robert "Scoop" Jackson

editor of The Agenda

edited by James Williams
forward by Goldie

IN DEDICATION...

One thing I've learned in doing rap shit - you gotta give props to those who deserve it. Here we go:

The Family, of course. Just a quick thanx for sticking by me. The Fellas for not making feel like I was "all that" because I went back to educate myself, and educate othas along the way. That really meant alot. To Chuck Money, for unconsciously challenging me to push for academic excellence. To Dashiki for thinking bigger than I probably would have. To my Tick Doooog Rollie. Thanks for keeping me on my toes, and my head into the "real" rap cuts. YaNoWhatImSayin'? And 2 Towns, 4 alternative Strong Island/side kick support. Peace, God.

I'd really like to thank the people who either didn't think I could do this, or really didn't give a shit. For real. You are part of the reason I got this done.

The last strong shout goes out to everybody down with The I (Strong Island) and at Howard University. And I do mean everybody! For the support, the encouragement, the honesty, and the education. Not just in school, but in all aspects of life. I've grown alot, and I owe each and everyone of you.

That's it. If I missed anybody, I still love ya! I busted my ass to get this book done. I don't know if it's done the right way, but it is done to the point where I'm satisfied with it. Understand there are 3 sides to every story told nowadayz - and the media tells two of them. Creating culture is not easy (that is why white folks have never done it). There is a

politically conscious, culturally aware, liberated, nationalistic, Black survival-kit side to rap music that is
being seriously overlooked. My job is to acknowledge their contributions, discuss our future together,
and counter what "others" have already written. This
book is done for both academia, and the brothas on the
block. This music is our music. It came from the block, and
it should stay on the block! So basically the book is the
TRUTH.

Special thanxx to Chuck D. for the Strong Island
support. To BET for the opportunity. And to Spike Lee for
proving that hard work sometimes does pay off for Black
people.

I dedicate this book to Momz for making me feel
like I always do right. To Ga-Ga; I think about you
everyday. To myself for surviving the accident, and taking
advantage of my second chance. My brother, Jack. My
Dad, Son. My Aunt Barbara. My Uncle Clif. And of course,
my wife Red. Much love. Last Shout goes to Pep Patty
(Tracey Sargent); I Love You, I miss you, and it's because
of you I was able to continue...

C-YA	Justice
Peace	I'm Gone
Outtie	I'm Ghost
Ah Right Then!	5000 G.
Stay Black	
	Scoop

US Library of Congress Catalog Card Number: 93-86397

The Last Black Mecca: Hip Hop
Robert 'Scoop' Jackson

First PUBLISHED IN USA, Britain and Trinidad
by Research Associates and Frontline Dist. Int'l Inc.

751 East 75th Street
Chicago, Illinois 60619
Fax: (312) 651-9850

UK office and Distributors: Karnak House
300 Westbourne Park Road
London W11 1EH
England
Tel. 071-221-6490

Typesetting Produced by: Laurem Business Center

TABLE OF CONTENTS

I. Preface

Chapter 1 * An Introduction To An African-American Phenomenon 1

Chapter 2 * "Doin' The Knowledge, B." 6

Chapter 3 * Definition Of A Hip Hop Culture 11

Chapter 4 * Black Out 18

Chapter 5 * Lyrical Content and Radical Analysis 27

Chapter 6 * Lyrical Content and Racial Analysis 36

Chapter 7 * "I'd Rather B Here 2 Xercize Tha Mind" 45

Chapter 8 * Intellectual Vietnam 50

Chapter 9 * A State Of Yo! 57

Chapter 10 * The Ghetto Code 67

Chapter 11 *A Black To The Future Agenda 74

Chapter 12 * On A Mission With No Permission 77

Chapter 13 *The Epilogue: Dope Fiction or Butter Politics? 84

II. References 100

THE LAST BLACK MECCA

Preface

When I began this project the relationship between rap music and the Black community was unfolding. No Rodney King, no "free" Mandela, no LA riots, no Clarence Thomas, no Menace II Society, and no Snoop Doggy Dogg. In 1989 the new Black consciousness movement was beginning to take shape. Jesse Jackson was moving to DC, Spike Lee had just dropped Do The Right Thing, and Biz had the "vapors". Basically things were simple then. The only people paying attention to Black people were...Black people.

In 4 years Black life has changed. America has experienced the darkside and rap is/was a big part of it. Along with over-extensive media attention, rap has gone glock (guns) and blunt (drugs) crazy. The original hip hop vibe has taken a direction towards the exploitation of Black human destruction instead of Black human salvation. And as much as any true b-boy or down-brotha wants to "represent", it is very hard to defend the positivity in this new direction.

The other area of rap that had gone unnoticed was in academia. In 1989 there were very few (a grave understatement) studies done on rap as a creative culture, or means of communication. The division between the MC and the professor was larger than the economic distance between Blacks and whites during the Reagan/Bush era. "Straight up noise", is how the scholars of the pre-thirty something generation used to refer to rap. The question I was always asked by them was, "Why study something that has no substance?". Now I went to a Black university (Howard), so don't get the impression that it was a "white thing" to reject rap; "colored" folks was doin' it too.

In 1993 that has also changed. There have been several books published in relation to rap (the two most recent by Kwanzi Kunjufu and Houston Baker) and how it impacts the society we live in. There have even been a few white writers who have "felt the need" to contribute to a culture that they are so far removed from they wouldn't know the difference between Rob Base and Onyx. But if it will sell - they will write it.

The importance of indoctrinating the history and significance of "true rap" and "true hip hop" comes with true representation. for once, in literature, hip hop is rightfully REPRESENTED. The author of this book has been to the Latin Quarters, has seen KRS freestyle, has Chuck Chillout and Red Alert on the mix, and has been "down with the kings" (Run DMC) before they dropped "Rock Box". In other words, THIS AIN'T NO FRONT.

It was once said that the true story of hip hop will never be told because nobody <u>can</u> write it. Yeah a few articles will be written in The Source, but according to a large majority of white and middle class African-americans, nobody in hip hop was educated or "versed" enough to put it in the context of something bounded instead of stapled. Wrong! From the dl to C-Lo, this book truly represents hip hop the way it was meant to be rep'ed by a brotha who is willing to die for the shit. Good or bad, that is all anybody can ask when they are in search of information, knowledge and the truth. And basically that is what this book is all about.

The last area of concern that can not be overlooked (because it really is not thoroughly discussed in the book) is the post-NWA era in hip hop.When focusing on the positive aspects and pro-social potential hip hop has as a shaper of minds and a communicative force, it is very difficult to explain the vocal activity that has embraced the "soul" of rap now. It has become a challenge to "hold up" the songs of Public Enemy when Compton's Most Wanted and MC Eiht are going gold and platinum. The role of society becoming more violently open has had a direct effect on the marketing and managing of rap and rap music. It is becoming a problem because of the glorification that has now come with the territory of "blowing a niggaz head off" on wax.

The power of money (and the fact that record companies push this type of product harder than they do a "regular" rap release) is what constitutes the poetry.

THE LAST BLACK MECCA

Artists have become "rappers" instead of MC's. No longer does an artist in rap try to "move the crowd", his or her job has now come down to selling units and maybe, just maybe, make a good song or record. And as stated in Chapter 11 of this book, "ghetto darwinism" has become the rap artists' true association with survival. Living in a world where you have no control (after you sign that contract) and you have no lawyer, as an artist you do what you gotta do and say what they want you to say to keep your career in check and alive. God bless 'em though, because hopefully "the beats" will come back in style and LL and Moe Dee will battle for pleasure and talent display, instead of Dre and Luke for money and record sales.

Rap, rap music and hip hop are all a part of the new American culture. What has to be remembered is that they are all created by young Black minds for young Black people. As a creative culture we have to sometimes look beyond the surface to find the true relevance in what it is we are doing and what it is we have created. Too broke to buy instruments, young Black men created a tool that would change the face of America. Rap is the gift this Black generation is giving. And even though it sometimes gets out-of-hand, it is a very special and honorable gift. And above and beyond anything else (and I don't care how you want to look at it) rap has done two major things: 1) ignited the re-emergence of Malcolm X, and 2) got Martin Luther King a holiday in Arizona. That by themselves are feats worthy of honest recognition - and that is what the following pages are all about. So please read carefully because from the looks of the direction society is going, rap may be the last Black voice you will ever hear.

Peace,

Goldie

THE LAST BLACK MECCA

CHAPTER 1

An Introduction To An African-American Phenomenon

"Music is the primary transmitter of our culture. The artists are free to express themselves. Music at its best relieves us, revives us - it so often informs us, and it sometimes renews us. Rap music may be the most phenomenal break towards the expression of culture since jazz, as an art form. Rap music is here to stay, and to see the youth pick up the bits and pieces of life as it is lived, and transform mess into a message, and be able to uplift people, is a phenomenal art form."

-Jesse Jackson, 1989

THE LAST BLACK MECCA

Music is a symbolic function of culture. It functions as a symbolic part of life in that it does represent other things (Merriam, 1964). Music helps unify social collectives, introduce new topics, teaches norms and rules, and creates new symbols. In the Black/African-American community, rap music is a teaching process and a reflection at the same time. The African-american community is a highly diversified, interrelated aggregate of people who unite into relatively cohesive structures in response to white and government oppression, racism, and patterned repression (Blackwell, 1975). Through this music, young Black males have created an innovative source of communication that presents an oral history of a brutalized generation.

The musical culture that has come from African-americans is the most profound sound of the 20th century. From Jelly Roll Morton to Scott Joplin to Gil Scott Heron to Rakim, it is all in the same continuum. Rap (or Hip Hop as it is more formally called because of its' relation to the Be Bop/jazz era) music related to what Charlie Parker and Thelonious Monk did because it came from the city's poorest area, out of miserable public education, out of miserable housing, and made something out of very little. In some way this bothers a large portion of white society, the media, and a segment of upper and middle-class African-americans who attempt to intellectualize rap music, and stamp it with a seal of triviality and disapproval. Black youth have created something that has affected the whole world in terms of rhythm, movement, the spoken word, and the visual art.[1]

African-americans are becoming educated and informed though a form of communication over which white society has no immediate control. Feeling threatened the media continuously attempts to write off an entire culture by making this artistic expression synonymous with dangerous, harmful activities. In turn, a majority of upper and middle-class Black people disassociate themselves with rap music, regard it as noise, and consider it threatening and primitive. While economic and psychological disparity between middle-class and poor African-americans continues to grow, white entertainment outlets consistently defeat Black institutions for the loyalty of Black audiences (George, 1988).

Rap music/Hip Hop culture is a movement of liberation. Lyrics in most rap songs are reflective of the situation that faces Blacks in America on a daily basis. Rap is an expression of alienation and oppression. It attempts to direct the anger of the Black youth, and combine the formula of "nommo" and bragadoccio, and transform messages that have the potential to entertain, educate and promote information as to what is going on in different neighborhoods, and communicate it at a rate of speed never heard or seen before.

African-americans will have to meet their own needs by living up to, and supporting, our own

4

rhetoric. Rap music has taken the responsibility of formulating constructive knowledge, and transforming it into a communicative force. Rap music enables young African-americans to challenge information. It finds people that are able to communicate and connects them with those that are unable to communicate with the rest of the world. Rap is Black America's television station. It gives a whole perspective of what exists, and what Black life is all about (Ridenhour, 1988). Rap music has the potential to extend beliefs that music has an impact at physical, emotional, and cognitive levels (Lull, 1985) As a form of edutainment (education and entertainment) rap music has the potenial for redirecting the attitudes and ideologies of many African-americans by giving a complete reflection of the social and psychological reality that is the everyday experience within the Black community.

CHAPTER 2

DOIN' THE KNOWLEDGE, B. : Using Albert Bandura's "Social Learning Theory" To Examine The Pro-Social Messages In Rap

"The history of the American Negro is the history of (this) strife, this longing to attain self-conscious manhood, to merge his double self into a better and truer self . In this merger he wishes neither of the old selves to be lost. He would not Africanize America, for America has too much to teach the world and Africa. He would not bleach his Negro soul in a flood of white Americanism, for he knows that Negro blood has a message for the world. He simply wishes to make it possible for a man to be both Negro and American" (Du Bois, 1903).

External influences affect human attitudes and human behavior. In the Social Learning Theory, Albert Bandura, emphasizes the prominent roles played by symbolic and self-regulartory processes in psychological functioning. Social learning approaches human behavior in terms of "a continuous reciprocal interaction between cognitive, behavioral, and enviromental determinents" (Bandura, 1977). the Value of a theory is ultimately judged by the power of the procedures it generates to effect psychological changes. Theories must demonstrate predictive power. In the Social Learning Theory, Bandura claims people vary in what they teach, model, amd reinforce with children. Part of this book will use Bandura's premises to examine the power of popular music to create socially shared meanings by exploring and celebrating in a state of awareness or consciousness that which a particular audience identifies with as an expression of its emotional and moral precepts (Chesboro, Foulger, Nachman,and Yannelli,1985).

7

Related studies have shown that Black adolescents are race-related when choosing musical styles for their listening. Black students choose rhythm and blues extensively. This single choice of music type suggests that for Black adolescents rhythm and blues is attractive because it helps them identify with Black traditions (MacConkey, 1974). Urban pre-school children are very likely to be exposed to rap music on a consistent basis, and probably find the music enjoyable. The lyrics rhyme, have rhythm, and are repetitious. Consequently, they are easy to learn through daily practice which sometimes occurs from frequent exposure. It is this oral rhythmic comunication's energy, repetition, rhythm, and mnemonic style that makes it successful in reaching urban youth, to the point that they can frequently articulate the lyrics verbatim (Hicks, 1987). Rap music presents African-American youth with a communicative vehicle of cultural familiarity and positive representation. Social learning can be adequately

used as a framework on which rap music, and its
potential, can be judged.

Learning by reinforcement (constant, repeti-
tive listening) is commonly portrayed as a mechanis-
tic process in which responses are shaped automatically and unconsciously by their immediate consequences. Simple actions can be altered by their
effects without awareness of the relationship between actions and outcomes (Bandura, 1977). Sub-
sequently rap music can be held partially responsible
for the public re-emergence of the Afrocentric ideology that exists today in many African-american communities. Through changes in lyrics, messages in
numerous rap songs focused on political awareness,
government oppression, police brutality (George,
1989), and the uplifting of cultural identity. This has
given the members in the Black community a chance
to find identification through a different form of communication.

Social learning theory defines negative self-

9

concepts in terms of proneness to devalue oneself, and positive self-concepts as a tendency to judge one's self favorably (Bandura, 1977). African-Americans, through-out history, have been unable to receive messages consistently in order to develop thorough positive self-concepts. Therefore the messages that originate from African-american communities and neighborhoods are vital messages, with the potential to bring about strong, positive self-concepts. It is through these messages that self-negativism, and negative self-concepts, can begin to be erased in many of America's Black communities. In the '30's these messages came from Black men who struggled to find a way to feed, and keep their families alive. In the '60's these messages came from political and civil activists who were determined to achieve racial equality. In the '90's these messages are coming from urban area youths (young men and women) that are destined to ignite, and teach, cultural achievement and pride.

CHAPTER 3

Definition of a Hip Hop Culture

"Descending from the tribes of Africa, inspired by great Black leaders. We are the coming of the God's new drum. In Africa we communicated with the drum. We are descended from one. We still communicate with the drum, but it's a futuristic drum."

J. Hunter, 1990

Hip Hop is where that futuristic drum can be found. Before the term "rap" was placed on the next form of African music, hip hop music had become a culture within the Black community. It was through hip hop music that rap was formed.

In the late 1940's a revolution of music called "be-bop" emerged from the Black community. The music, unleashed at the dawn of World War II, was the voice of repressed, Black Americans finally boiling to the surface. The feverish rhythmic drive, the careening melodic leaps, and the harmonic progressions tilting on the edge of atonality, resurrected the predominant language of jazz; and ignited the careers of such visionaries as Dizzy Gillespie, Max Roach, Charlie Parker, Kenny Clarke, Roy Haynes, Archie Shepp, John Coltrane, Ornette Coleman, and Cecil Taylor (Reich,1990; Kofsky,1970). No other form of expression so radically altered the direction of American jazz, and no other musical language has succeeded in supplanting it (Reich,1990). The complexity, anger, and defiance of be-bop represented nothing less than a clinched fist raised skyward. Hip hop has become the modern reproduction of the be-bop era. It, hip hop, is the reproduction of the world, only on vinyl and under the ordering of a coherent mind (Watrous,1990).

In the mid-70's, in New York City, young

Definition of a Hip Hop Culture

Blacks pioneered a new type of music by prolonging the break (drum beat) sections of different records while playing them at house parties, community centers, and in the parks. Afrika Bambaataa, DJ Kool Herc, and Grandmaster Flash are responsible for generating large attractions to the music, and were instrumental in developing a form of music that has always been present in some form in Black music. Afrika Bambaataa, leader of the Zulu Nation (a non-violent organization comprised of Black and Latin rappers, dancers, graffiti artists, and fans) circulated tapes, and preached a positive message through bootleg records of his; which are considered the first hip hop recordings. Grandmaster Flash was more interested in using the turntables and mixer as instrument. Over his scratching techniques and "virtuoso" mixing, the microphone would be left open for budding MC's (masters of ceremony / mic controllers) to recite lyrical poetry. The way "rappers" rhymed over the music of the deejays was derived from Jamacian reggae sound systems (Needs,1989), which was a part of DJ Kool Herc's culture.

The roots and forerunners of this culture can be traced further back than the warm summers in the South Bronx. There were underground activities that would turn out to be the forerunners of the rap style. Poetress of the Black experience Nikki Giovanni set her dark verse to jazz and funk backdrops, while The Last Poets, in 1970, rallied against white oppression, accused Blacks of laziness and escape through drugs, and zeroed in on the social ills of society with vocal venom and little more than the beat of a conga drum (Needs, 1989; Needs, 1989). Abiodum Oyewole, David Jordan Nelson, Alafia Pudim, Omar Ben Hussen, and Nilaja (the original members of The Last Poets) spoke of a revolution coming in New York that would see " Jesus Christ standing on the corner of Lenox Avenue and 125th Street trying to catch the first gypsy cab out of Harlem". At the same time, The Black Voices preached with similar consciousness in

Watts. Songs such as "I'll Stop Calling You Nigger" and "Response To A Bourgeois Nigger" chastised Blacks for falling victim to drugs, and promoted fierce pride in recognizing the accomplishments of Malcolm X, John Coltrane, and Nina Simone. Later people, such as Gil Scott Heron, H. Rap Brown, and Eldridge Cleaver set the tone for the nationalistic ideology that has influenced the entire hip hop culture.

In the latter part of the 1970's the emphasis on lyrics began to replace the musical aspects that were the concrete foundation of hip hop. In 1978, the Fatback Band and the Sugarhill Gang recorded rap records that gained the attention of many African-Americans in the country. The songs were about partying, and having a good time. Four years later Grandmaster Flash and the Furious Five (featuring Melle Mel and Duke Booty) recorded "The Message". The song painted a vivid picture of life on the streets, and in the Black community. It was a powerful song that was considered an "urban nightmare that was all too real" (Winthorpe, 1988). The next five years hip hop music took many turns. An association, as well as a division with rap music grew evident. Herman, Kelly, and Life's "Dance To the Drummer's Beat" and "Planet Rock/Looking For The Perfect Beat" by Afrika Bambaataa and the SoulSonic Force became historical in the advent of hip hop, but the emergence of rap groups Run-DMC, the Treacherous 3, Hurt Em' Bad, Funky 4 + 1, the Crush Crew, the Rakes, Whodini, and LL Cool J bought the lyric into the foreground. Many other groups emerged, and millions of records were sold. The theme of rap during this time was self-gratification, and musical enjoyment. The influence of "The Message" was not felt again until 1987 with the release of Yo! Bum Rush The Show by Public Enemy.

SoulSonic Force set the standard for hip hop by allowing producers the chance to effectively create "breaks" which could be programmed to continue indefinitely behind the rapper's voice. Run-DMC was

Definition of a Hip Hop Culture

instrumental in the development of the "hard" rap style, which was musically stripped down to drum machines, scratches, and voices (They were also influential in collaborating rock guitar riffs with the sequencing of drum beats which was responsible for introducing many white Americans to the art form of rap, and at the same time introducing a larger Black audience to "rhythmic" rock and roll.) Public Enemy combined both elements and used innovative sampling techniques, a Black nationalistic ideology, and socially conscious and constructive lyrics to bring the hip hop culture into the 1990's with preparation, direction, and spirituality. Through Public Enemy, hip hop has become a repository for nearly all recorded information.

Note: The author failed to mention , but did not forget, Eric B. and Rakim, whose Paid In Full album was directly responsible for placing James Brown and other rhythm and blues legends into the core of existing rap sampling. Without their masterful productions, Rakim's (arguably the best MC ever) delivery, and their Muslim beliefs (the Five Percent Nation), rap music may have fallen victim to an American pop culture, and lost the Black following essential to the survival of hip hop.

THE LAST BLACK MECCA

CHAPTER 4

BLACK OUT: Media, Society, and Rap Music

One function of communication is to provide intelligence about what the other elite is doing, and about its strength. Fearful that intelligence channels will be controlled by the other, in order to withhold and distort, there is a tendency to resort to secret surveillance. Efforts are made to "black out" the self in order to counteract the scrutiny of the potential enemy. In addition, communication is employed affirmatively for the purpose of establishing contact with audiences within the frontiers of the other power (Lasswell,1948). In America, African-americans are this audience. Limited control of media services, and outlets, hinders African-Americans

18

from establishing a communicative base central in providing information. There is no national Black newspaper, national Black television network, national Black radio network, or Black production and film distribution company that fosters to the greater need of African-Americans across the country. There needs to be communication outlets available for Blacks to utilize mass distribution systems, or technology to disseminate preselected editorial content to the public (Johnson, 1989).

Rap music is one of the only central means of communication available to the larger portion of African-American society that dispenses information, and messages, essential in expanding the Black voice in this country.

Because of this, the media (radio, television, and print) have collectively attempted to diminish the entire hip hop culture as "a paranoid diatribe poisoned with plainly racist language"

(Gunderson, 1990). In March 1990 (and again in June 1992), *Newsweek* magazine ran a cover story on the rap attitude. The authors claimed that rap is primarily "a working-class and under-class phenomenon, a response to the diminishing expectations of millions of American youths who forgot to go to business school in the 1980's"[1]. In 1989 the FBI publicly printed a letter in the *Village Voice* directed to Jerry Heller, the manager of rap group N.W.A., about the song "F_ _ _ Tha Police". The Anti-Defamation League protested against the lyrics in many Public Enemy records. Claiming lyrics anti-Semitic, the ADL launched a media crusade to protest the existence of Public Enemy and their music. Even television gave way by the visual exposure given to The 2 Live Crew when they were bought to court on obscenity charges. By consistently running follow-up stories, television (with the assistance of radio, and print) successfully painted an image of obscenity and associated it solely with rap music. And more recently, the all-out-govern-ment-included crusade on Ice T about the hard rock (not rap) song, "Cop Killer".

The image the media has painted of rap music is one of a bombastic, self-aggrandizing music, that is notorious and is "as scary as sudden footsteps in the dark" [2]. This portrayal has hindered the perception and acceptance of rap music amongst members of Black society. Black media does not promote it, Black radio upper and middle class Blacks do not listen to it. All of these behavioral activitie can be attributed to the role the mass media played in shaping the country's perception of rap music.

In every social system there is a prin-ciple motif, a primordial center of interest which is always ideological and material, and is recognized and approved by members of the group who are under a moral organization in this social covenant (Ellul,1969). Activating self-punishment or creating

self-produced distress that motivates various individuals to defensive actions (Bandura, 1977) is the
mechanism used by the media to disassociate Black
establishments with messages of African-american
communication. White society has consciously im-
posed demands upon Blacks that are psychologically and socio-economically unattainable in this
country. Therefore, anytime a socially conscious,
morally correct member of African descent vocally
acknowledges his or her beliefs, and realizes the
implications he or she is being put up against - they
are controlled. Their accomplishments are demeaned,
and their voices are regulated.   This society is
designed to suppress the importance of Blacks. This
situation has caused Blacks to doubt their self importance and become critical of each other
(Bolden,1989). This is what is happening to rap
music and the entire hip hop movement. The media
and white society has found a way to regulate the
expansion of rap music by informing segments of

22

Black society that the music has no redeeming social value, is negative, self-assertive, and angry.

Many Blacks accept this, and have no way of challenging this perception without hearing the product. Yet, the main vehicle (Black radio) in promoting the product (rap) is void in doing so because it refuses to associate with the product. According to Terri Avery, Program Director of KMJQ Houston, rap records have short life spans, "which ultimately affects the sales and also reinforces the 'novelty' aspects to advertisers".

Black radio simply isn't supporting rap music wholeheartedly. Both Black and pop radio tend to treat rap as a second-class art form - a passing trend. A Chicago radio station, which caters to Black adults, totes an "absolutely no rap" slogan to publicize their programming. It is ironic that a radio station would denounce any type of music, but choosing to publicly denounce rap music to their adult audience is definitely a slap in the face to Black youth (Bolden,1989).

THE LAST BLACK MECCA

In our society today information occupies a central position, and assumes a dimension that is both pervasive and omnipotent. Information has been perceived as having the power to influence individual, as well as collective behavior, and to engender personal and collective uncertainty, thus guiding our decisions on issues close to or remote from our environment (Lippmann, 1932; Lang and Lang,1981; Gandy,1982; Graber,1984). In the Social Learning Theory, self produced distress creates the conditions for the development of various forms of deviant behavior (Bandura,1977). Society has also paralleled Black youth with, deviant behavior and activities. As far as rap music is concerned, society and the media have found a way to not recognize groups, such as Boogie Down Productions, Public Enemy, the Jungle Brothers, X Clan, Eric B. and Rakim, Queen Latifah, Arrested Development, De La Soul, Kool Moe Dee, Big Daddy Kane, Professor Griff, Gang Starr, Def Jef, Paris, the Intelligent Hoodlum, the Brand Nubians, The Dismasters, King Sun, Isis, Main Source, Stetsasonic, YZ, Ten Tray, the Defiant Giants, Digital Underground, 2Pac, Lakim Shabazz, Prince Akeem, A Tribe Called Quest, Del The Funkee Homosapien, Naughty By Nature, Heavy D., Chubb Rock, Pete Rock and C.L. Smooth, Showbiz & AG, Diamond D., Black Sheep, Nefertiti, Yaggfu Front, L.O.N.S., Puba, Breed, Kam, Lords Of The Underground, Digable Planets, EPMD, Das Efx, The Coup, Masta Ace and Sister Souljah; and exploit The 2 Live Crew, N.W.A., Snoop Doggy Dog, and Ice T. Raps rapid proliferation and appeal to growing audiences sends shivers of panic through more than a few alarmists (Gundersen,1990), and because of rap's popularity, the Black subculture is becoming part of Middle America; and this is scary to many white people who grew up not relating to Blacks (Kot,1990).

The messages presented by the afore-mentioned groups are ones that place an emphasis on African and African-american knowledge and awareness, self-sufficiancy and global recognition, which has become the standard in hip hop today. In general, the media has manipulated the facts to get across an agenda. It has basically given an inaccurate portrayal of a music that fosters itself on being culturally specific. Rap music, as a whole, has become a dissertation on Black pride and unity, and a reflection on society through the eyes of young Blacks in America. By not recognizing projects and records by the Stop The Violence Movement (a group of successful rap artists created a universal organization, and recorded a record that spoke out on Blacks overcoming self-destruction), and singling out acts like, The Geto Boys and Dr. Dre, the media continues to not judge the music, but judge the character and surroundings that embrace the music.

CHAPTER 5

Lyrical Content and Radical Analysis

My forefather was a king
He wore fat gold chains, and fat ruby rings
Nobody believes this to be true
Maybe it's because my eyes ain't blue.
You ain't gon' find it in your history book
Come here young brother and take a look
You dig down deep inside this hard cover
Don't you know you was barred my brother.
                                              Jungle Brothers
from "Acknowledge Your Own History"

In the cognitive control section of the Social Learning Theory, Bandura discusses the value language symbols which serve as vehicles of thought. Thinking depends to a large extent upon language symbols. Thinking also occurs in terms of numerical and musical notations, and other symbols. By manipulating symbols that convey relevant information, one can gain an understanding of casual relation-

ships, create new forms of knowledge, solve problems, and deduce consequences without actually
performing any activities (Bandura,1977). These symbols provide instruments of thought. Operations for
processing information, people can formulate alternative solutions and evaluate the probable and long
range consequences of different courses of action
(p. 173). This is the element of language development which human thought is linguistically based.
Identifying rap lyrics in this aspect will better equip
the reader in understanding the structure and function of rap music in the theoretical perspective of
shaping social values.

The lyrics presented earlier are from "Acknowledge Your Own History" by the Jungle Brothers. The lyrics in that song, and many others, are
indicative of the direction rap music is taking to raise
the consciousness level of its listening audience.
Chuck D., leader of the group Public Enemy, explains the attempt, through his lyrics, to show Blacks

the necessity of fostering self-pride.

"We came out in 1987, and one of my first objectives was to lessen the quest for materialism in Black people, especially Black brothers. My goal is to build 5000 new Black leaders through my means of communication who will ensure that Blacks remain focused on the most crucial societal issues confronting the Black race in the '90's. Rap serves as the communication that they (Blacks) don't get for themselves to make them feel good about themselves.

"Rap is Black America's TV station. It gives a whole perspective of what exists, and what Black life is all about. And Black life doesn't get the total spectrum of information through anything else. They don't get it through print because kids won't pick up magazines, or books, really unless it's got pictures of rap stars. They don't see themselves on TV. Rap is the *Headline News*.

" I got 60 minutes to do it on an album, then it's over. How much teaching can you do in 60 minutes?

(That's why) I call myself a dispatcher of information. I name important people, places, dates, and I spark enough curiosity so the listener can begin the search and research." [3]

This thought process has become almost holistic in the ideology of rap today. The rap profession has been a major force in African-americans understanding of their present and past. Through lyrics, young Blacks have been exposed to the words of Sony Carson, W. E. B. DuBois, and Marcus Garvey. The voices of Martin Luther King Jr., and Malcolm X Can be heard in many rap songs. Producers use excerpts from their speeches as "samples" to enhance the concepts of messages in the songs. Rap gives Black children the opportunity to learn about their culture and heritage through the lyrics of the songs. In essence, rap combines social messages with Black nationalistic overtones.

Not all rap songs fall into the category of raising social consciousness. Rap music has the

Lyrical Content and Radical Analysis

tendency to be alarming and sometimes quite controversial. Along with covering issues concerning social situations within the Black community, rap music has glorified violence, encouraged polygamy, and belittled women. It is this area of the music that critics have been quick to denounce positive elements of rap as unfocused. Outside of this small minority of rap artists who are void of producing socially responsible material, the rap music industry is filled with lyric writers focused on "uplifting the mind".

Five of the more popular groups in the Black community among rap artists are Boogie Down Productions, X Clan, Eric B. and Rakim, the Jungle Brothers, and Public Enemy. Record sales among African-americans indicate that these five groups are the front-runners in this arena of hip hop. In 1990 these groups combined record sales of over 14 million. [4] According to the recently released Census report there are 30 million African-americans, or people of African descent, in this country. 36 percent fall between the ages of 5 years old and 24 years old (the general age of education, and the age area in which the primary number of record buyers of rap music falls). These numbers indicate the strong support of these groups, as well as a large listening audience (especially in the Black community since not one of their albums entered the Billboard Top 20 album chart in 1989, but all surpassed the top 20 on Billboard's Black Album chart). The lyrical focus of these groups centers around cultural and social awareness. A better understanding of the lyrical content needs to be made by taking an in-depth listen to these selected songs by the groups cited earlier:

Welcome To The Terrordome by Public Enemy
Fight The Power by Public Enemy
Move The Crowd by Eric B. & Rakim
In The Ghetto by Eric B. & Rakim

Lyrical Content and Radical Analysis

Black Man In Effect by Boogie Down Productions (BDP)

You Must Learn by Boogie Down Productions (BDP)

Funkin' Lesson by XClan

Raise The Flag by XClan

Beed On A String by Jungle Brothers

Black Woman by Jungle Brothers

In examining the lyrics of these songs, the listener will find many symbols of African-American heritage mentioned. Nat Turner, Martin (Luther King Jr.), Adam (Clayton Powell), Malcolm (X), Huey (Newton) were all mentioned in the verse of "Funkin'" Lesson" by X Clan. KRS-One sends a duel message out to both a Black and white audience in "Black Man In Effect". White society has built up their race on the concept of violence, and conquering, yet they refuse to hear the Black man speak. To compensate, he calls for equality in education. Science verses silence. Rakim's lyrics are more introspective. He preaches of external lessons being learned by using the "third eye", which is the eye of wisdom. A travel through the Asiatic (original man) mind. "From knowledge born, to knowledge precise", covers all knowledge conceived from birth up to the present day. The Jungle Brothers reach for the finding of an African syndrome through "the vibe". The vibe is their music. Every lyric touches on an area of connecting positive self-concepts and hip hop music. Public Enemy's message is much more direct. Intellectual violence over physical violence. Rap music originates from areas of aggression. The harshness of the lyrics are indicative of the products of the environment, as well as the environment of the product. Non-passive messages and intellect have to become correlated for the messages to be absorbed by the listener.

The absorbing of such information, according

Lyrical Content and Radical Analysis

to the Social Learning Theory, can affect behavior and attitudes through intermediary cognitive processes. By manipulating symbolically the information that is derived from experience, one can comprehend events and generate new knowledge about them (Bandura,1977). The lyrical content of these songs strongly suggest that individuals (Black people) challenge the existing information, and look at the surroundings, the self, the culture, and create motivational goals for positive self-evaluation. Once individuals have made self-satisfaction contingent upon goal attainment, they tend to persist in their efforts until their performances match what they are seeking to achieve (Bandura,1977). These five groups, along with numerous other rap artists, are trying to ignite a social awareness that will construct goal attainment in the Black community.

CHAPTER 6

Lyrical Content and Racial Analysis

In the spiritual strivings section of "The Souls of Black Folk", Du Bois discusses the fact that there is no true American music except the wild sweet melodies of the Negro slave, and the significance of education to real life, social responsibilities, and the meaning of progress. These issues are addressed in many rap songs, and provide instruments for thought: How does it feel to be a problem? Being a problem is a strange experience - particularly even for one who has never been anything else (Du Bois, 1903). Slavery was indeed the sum of all villianies, the cause of sorrow, the root of all prejudice. He (the slave) began to have a dim feeling that, to attain his place in the world, he must be himself, and not another (Du Bois,1903). This is the element of race separation, true history and Black civilization which fosters the underlying nationalism in rap lyrics. Identifying rap lyrics in this aspect will better equip the reader in understanding the structure and function of rap music in the conceptual perspective of promoting self-reliance.

Kool Moe Dee's "Rise and Shine" (with guest appearances by KRS-One of Boogie Down Productions and Chuck D. of Public Enemy) establishes a new realm of awareness by incorporating three different concepts pertaining to Black life: wisdom (Moe Dee's lyrics), acceptability (KRS's lyrics), and responsibility (Chuck's lyrics). Songs such as these, and hard core "gangsta" rap songs have made some listeners refer to the music as a new species of blackface minstrelsy (Leland, 1992). As quoted from a Billboard magazine editorial in reference to rap music and its' audience, "The Chicken-thieving, razor-toting `coon of the 1890's is the drug-dealing, Uzi-toting `nigga of today...". It is these attitudes and statements that continually put rap music and artists on the defensive because the "attacks" are seemingly unjustified.

In dealing with lyrical content at this level it must be acknowledged that the relationship an artist has with the society in which he or she lives in general constitutes the lyrical material recorded. Music by no means can change societal behavior, but it does have the power to "spark curiosity" and instigate attitudes. The racial attitude in America right now is very tense. Rap music did not cause this, but it "reported" on it. From 1989 -1993 the racial attitudes of both the major races in this country has escalated to almost dangerous proportions. Incidents that have occurred involving Blacks and whites have caused the overall behavior of both races to change toward one another. Where rap was once fostering a new pride of Black awareness in 1989, it now, in 1993, makes direct points as to why things are the way they are, who is to blame, and what has to be done to "get

ours". The United States government, and white society-at-large, have become the target groups of todays rap ideology. The entire hip hop culture understands that concerted efforts have been made to examine the effects of images of Blacks as portrayed in the media and society; and that the message expressed in every form of communication, be it verbal, the printed word, or visual, has been that Blacks are inferior to whites in every way - intellectually, culturally,
economically, and technologically. This leaves whites helplessly superior in all ways, and reinforces the variety of anti-Black preconceptions (Howard, 1987).

The reflection of this attitude change is featured in the lyrics of a wide variety of songs released between 1990-92. More emphasis is being placed on the effective way white people have used racism to keep Black people in a particular "realm of darkness". A revolution is being forecast, and this new focus in rap and the lyrics were recorded **before** the Rodney King verdict and the "freedom fight" in Los Angeles. A better understanding of this lyrical content can be made by taking an in-depth listen to the selected songs by the groups cited earlier and a few new ones:

I Wanna Kill Sam by Ice Cube

Horny Lil Devil by Ice Cube

The Final Solution by Sister Souljah

Madness by Ten Tray

Pure Melanin by Defiant Giants

Verbal Intercourse by Proffesor Griff

Can't Truss It by Public Enemy

Who Stole The Stole by Public Enemy

Holy Rum Swig by XClan

Fire & Earth by XClan

Teach The Children by Eric B. & Rakim

Casualty of War by Eric B. & Rakim

Poisonous Products by BDP

Questions and Answers by BDP

Revolutionaries are forged through constant struggle and the study of revolutionary ideas and experiences (Forman, 1985). The Black hip hop artists of today are in many ways considered revolutionary because they represent voices of disenfranchised Blacks. A segment of society that rarely is spoken about on the 10 o'clock news or in the halls of Congress, and a message that most America would still rather ignore, if not censor (Kot,1991). Yet it is the total lack of understanding, combined with white supremist ideologies, fear of the truth, Black mental apathy and conservativism, and white society's domination of all communication mediums that make these lyrics seem so appalling and unjustified. In a recent Rolling Stone interview Ice T said, "Rap is really funny...But if you don't see that it's funny, it will scare the shit out of you."[5] If one does not walk the streets of the person screaming the loudest, one will

41

never comprehend the pain behind the scream.

An assessment of the songs:

Boogie Down Productions, Public Enemy, XClan and Eric B. & Rakim have set the standard for the concept change in the lyrical focus of hip hop. Instead of studying the original history of our people, they now stress the importance of also realizing the role whites (particularly the white man; aka: Jack, the Devil, Him, Einstein, John Hoodie, the Barbarian,etc.) have played in the suppressing of African people. Everything from the initial slave trade to the Black involvement in the Persian Gulf War is mentioned in the lyrics of their recent songs.

The "new crew", or group of artists bring a more direct, hard-edge, "let's turn the tables on the oppressor" style to the lyrical rap format. The ideologies of reparations, Mike McGee, and the 5% Nation are vividly evident in the lyrics of Sister Souljah, Ice

Cube, the Defiant Giants, Ten Tray, and Professor Griff. Where Ice Cube takes direct aim at the American government and media systems, Ten Tray strictly recites historical facts and events that have been detrimental in the forward movement of Black people, and warns any "guilty" listener that "revolution" (payback) is inevitable (emanate). The Defiant Giants make statements about the importance of understanding the genetic strength of pigmentation in all African people. The fact that Black people can reproduce all shades of people is instrumental in understanding the inferiority complex that whites have attained over the years. Professor Griff and Sister Souljah are both prophets from the group Public Enemy. The former in his lyrics gives "peace to the gods" and explains the concept of the 5% Nation (a doctrine, extending from Muslim teachings, that instills the knowledge of self, wisdom and understanding of the Asiatic man, and the teachings of Clarence 13X); while the latter is simply the "rebirth" of Angela Davis on wax. Born and raised "not to make white people feel comfortable", these artists have taken an "unindoctrinated pledge" to ignite mental (and possibly behavioral) action in the Black community. Self-esteem through music is great, but bringing forth the knowledge necessary to combat the forces that have plagued, and are continuing to plague, Black people around the world is the master key needed to unlock the dormat-minds of that area of Black society unwilling to separate itself from the white world for the betterment and advancement of our people (Jackson, 1992). The emergence of groups like Ten Tray, XClan, BDP, and artists like Griff, Souljah, and Cube are mandatory if the Black race plans on avoiding what has already been in progress for 5000 years - the Destruction of Black Civilization.

CHAPTER 7

"I'D RATHER B HERE 2 XERCIZE THA MIND"

To be a poor man is hard, but to be a poor race in a land of dollars is the very bottom of hardship (Du Bois, 1903). An understanding of the general lives of the two major racial elements in this country must be addressed in order to gain some type of insight on rap music and it's following. In Du Bois' statement, his reference to poverty and race are the combined elements that are reflective of Black life. Economic setbacks, institutionalized poverty and sectionalized racism directly play a part in the life of the members of the Black/African-american community. The majority of the white/Eurocentric populace do not live under these constraints or conditions. Being poor is not something that all African-americans have experienced - but living in poor conditions attributed to that economic status is something that all African-americans can closely relate. This element plays a crucial and significant role in subverting Black social existence, and the void within white society of the "mentality" behind rap music.

Black popular culture must be assiduously scrutinized if it is to yield answers to questions such as: What values are important to Black people; What role can the analysis of Black popular culture play in identifying those values; Is Black popular culture helping the Black masses to acquire knowledge, understanding, and skills that will enable them to bridge the cultural gap that keeps them in a subservient position (Swindell, 1986)? As mentioned previously, the attempt to intellectualize creativity derived from the Black community, society (particularly white society) often misses the entire meaning of how and what the rap/hip hop culture is , and what it does for and to African-americans.

The inner city origins of hip hop provides the

basis of its' "hardcore" rebellious flavor (Shomari,1992). White society, in general, has a difficult time truly understanding non-European culture - especially when the culture extends from African descent. This explains why hip hop culture is the exact opposite of Anglo-American cultural traditions (Shomari, 1992), and why it is so misinterpreted. When Rakim talks about the "exile of the original man. Astray of ways...hardtimes", and then says, "...I'd rather be here to exercise the mind", he is directly referring to the trials African people (the original man) has gone through (exile), and how to this day (hardtimes) he can withstand the scrutiny and learn, educate and be educated (exercise the mind). Because the majority of white global society hasn't been through the same "struggle". They read a totally different story than what is actually being told.

A very large portion of rap music goes misunderstood and misinterpreted, because the system and people who are attempting to understand and interpret it are not from a similar origin that gave hip hop it's birth. Economically poor , the Black community has always created art forms that reflect its' living conditions. There is nothing moderate about America's Black community, so why should others look for something moderate to come from it? Rap is a reflection and self-examination of the Black community, and the activities that occur in it. The ridicule and systematic humiliation, the distortion of fact, the cynical ignoring of the better and the boisterous welcoming of the worst, and the disdain of everything Black (Du Bois,1903) that white society places on this particular phenomena, quietly exposes the lack of understanding of the total Black culture. Hence, Black people are, on many occasions, "blamed" for a massive amount of global and societal despair. And because rap is the "new infant" introduced to the world by African/Black culture, an association with human destruction is automatically placed on the music. Until the class/socioeconomic tables are turned, the fear of a Black planet theory will always create this paranoid, negative perception, and lack of understanding. As Ice T, one of the revolutionary hip hop godfathers and rap artist, once said, "Rap is really funny. It's an editorial...a particular thought pattern. But if you don't see it as funny, it will scare the shit out of you". [1] As rap continues to "scare" thousands of people, young Black rap artists will continue to "exercise the minds" of millions who are exposed to the reality of Black life in America.

CHAPTER 8

INTELLECTUAL VIETNAM: Using W.E.B.Du Bois' "The Souls Of Black Folk"To Dissect The Hip Hop Mentality

I am African first, I am Black first
I want what's good for me and my people first
And if my survival means your total destruction, then so be it
You built this wicked system
They say two wrongs don't make it right
But it damn sure makes it even.
Sister Souljah from "The Hate That Hate Produced"

From the double life every American Negro must live, as a Negro and as an American, as swept on by the current of the nineteenth while yet struggling in the eddies of the fifteenth century - from this must arise a painful self-consciousness, an almost morbid sense of personality and moral hesitancy which is fatal to self-confidence. Such a double life, with double thoughts, double duties, and double social classes, must give raise to the double words and double ideas, and tempt the mind to pretense or to revolt, to hypocrisy or to radicalism (Du Bois,1903). Lives of dignity and honor can be and have been lived in a wide variety of political, economic, and technological circumstances. Contemporary society consists of an open-ended, multilayered texture of stories, many of which are contradictory and incommensurate with each other, for which individuals appropriate that which enables them to achieve coordination, coherence, and mystery. The skill with which individuals appropriate these stories varies, of course, and is directly related to the content of the stories they appropriate (Pearce, 1989). The second part of this book will deal with the concepts behind the activities surrounding and coming from the Black community, and use W.E.B. Du Bois' theory of duality, in his "The Souls Of Black Folk", as a concept for which Black people embrace rap music; and explain why vocal liberation continues to be an important facet in the life of African-americans.

The moral energies of the American people must be mobilized by new leadership intent on shaping both the existing and new political structures to deal with the emerging problems of urban America. None of these problems, physical or social, racial or cultural, is inherently solvable. The concept of "separate but equal" ghettoization is psychologically, politically, and judicially (since the Rodney King verdict) an impossible dream destined to become a nightmare for American society (Schuchter,1968). African-americans realize this and react. Rap music is one of the main reactors to comprehending the actuality of Black peoples situation in this country. Rebellious, revolutionary or trigger-happy, the majority of the Hip Hop culture mentally understand what DuBois meant by "ethical paradox". Halted on neans of unlimited advancement, but free to be American. In this situation the attitude of the "imprisoned group" may take three main forms: 1) a feeling of revolt or revenge; 2) an attempt to adjust all thought and action to the will of the greater group; or 3) a determined effort at self-realization and self-development despite enviroroning opinion (DuBois, 1903). The establishment of the rap culture embodies itself in these reactions.

The Black presence in America has always been typecast. The same role Blacks played socially in 1890 is the same role white society expects to be played in 1990: Subservient and withdrawn. Collectively rap has the strongest African voice in America. The coalition built by the young African-americans who represent a large segment of hip hop have taken the first step in rebuilding the psychological, political and social movement essential for total Black survival. The awareness of thedouble life forced upon members of Black society is the focus that underlies the life of rap music. the day of the scared,lip-trembling, word-changing, self-denying, comprominsing, knee-shaking Black people is over

(Souljah, 1992). Rap has created a new conscious form of Black cultural existence. The music, artists and lyrics havefilled a void reserved for black educators, politicians, clergymen, businessmen, and civic leaders. There are no limits to rap's manifestation. The fatalism that exists in the duality of the African-american can only be broken by separation. Rap often finds itself as the instigator generating the separation of the inhertied African within all Blacks and the monolithic American ideologies Black Americans have been raised on.

" The Souls Of Black Folk" accurately describes the trails faced by the anti-Negro establishment and the Negro. Radicalism or hypocritical compromise? Hip hop recreated the same belief by refusing to conform to pre-established norms and decided self-respect is worth more than the lands and houses; and people who voluntarily surrender such respect, or cease striving for it, are not worth civilizing (DuBois, 1903).

CHAPTER 9

A STATE OF YO!;
15 Years Of Stylee Change In Hip Hop; From Yo 2 Yo!

Evolution is the process of change. The rise of a nation, the pressing forward of a social class, means a bitter struggle, a hard and soul-sickening battle with the world such a few more favored classes know or appreciate (Du Bois,1903). The true form of any substance comes after it has evolved. Rap music has evolved, and it's truest form is hip hop (just as in the evolution of Black society, at the center, in it's truest form, rests the Black community). Rap music has gone through various periods of change - musically and socially. Many of these changes have come in the aftermath of societal change, and others have been at the forefront in directing the attitude of certain segments of society. African-american society has gone through the "bitter struggle, and hard, soul-sickening battles" to manifest an existing culture that is continuously at odds with itself. In these periods of evolution, value systems change. Attitudes, behavior and actions change. Outlooks change. The Hip Hop culture is no different. In order to sustain, expand and gain acceptability, artists constantly found new life by changing the lyrical, musical and mental direction of what is now called "hardcore hip hop".

It is very difficult to pin point what style was created originally in the era of hip hop. Lyrically, braggadocio and party themes were the mainstay in MC'ing. Then novelty (simple lyrics built around comedic substance) rap started to gain popularity. At all times rap artists (MC's) told stories about their everyday lives, their neighborhoods, and people they associated with. From Rodney Cee and Double K Rockwell's "Stoop Rap" to Pete Rock's freestyle intro to "On And On", rappers have always been able to paint a vivid picture of how they like to "kick It". But more important than the various lyrical styles that have been raised in the hip hop culture, it is the music - and the changes of styles - that is the foundation on which this phenomena exists.

In the early '70's the Temptations recorded a song entitled, "Ball Of Confusion". This song became important because it actually may have been the first song [recorded] that had both musical and lyrical rap undertones. Often overlooked by musical historians and rap researchers, "Ball Of Confusion" combined elements of pre-funk, soul, and harmony that is responsible for many of the track and sampling techniques used by numerous hip hop producers today. As the '80's rolled in, the music coming from the "underground" was strictly beats. With the invention of computer-programmed drum beats, artists found a very cost efficient and simplified way to record their songs. A wide variety of beats were created, and several hundred songs were recorded by a smaller number of groups. Studio time was low, and by only using drum beats (and occasionally a human beat box) young MC's were able to produce community acceptable music, and create a product that would not compete or be confused with R&B (rhythm & blues). Basically the "stripping down" of the music gave rap an identity it needed to survive on it's own standards. Then came Whodini...

In 1982 Ecstacy, Jalil, and Grandmaster Dee (with Larry "King of the Beat" Smith on production) recorded what at the time became the national anthem for the Burroughs. "Magic's Wand" not only created a new musical avenue (r&b / synthesized funk beats and grooves) for rap, but also helped WBLS radio/rap show personality, Mr. Magic, expand his underground popularity to "infamous" proportions. Everything after that release, from the "Haunted House Of Rock" to "Yours For The Night" to "Escape" to "The Freaks Come Out At Night" to

"Fugitive" to " One Love" to "Now That Whodini's In Tha Joint" was greatly responsible for exalting rap music into a contemporary Black culture, due to the fact that Whodini was one of the very few groups (along with Mantronix and UltraMagnetic) to fuse forms of rhythm & blues and dance-oriented sounds into their music - and still be "hard" enough to maintain the hip hop following (especially in New York) necessary for any rap crew. Arista records was financially secure enough to keep session musicians available for Whodini projects so that the basis of their music would be recorded by non-prerecorded material. That trend (if it actually was one) changed in 1986 with the world's introduction to Eric B. and Rakim. As vocalist and producer on hip hop's most forceful debut ever (Naughty By Nature's debut is second, and Dr. Dre's maybe third), "Eric B. is President" / "My Melody", Rakim and Eric composed a def, culturally resonant, un-pretentious art statement; one that forecasted the

61

"dopidity" of their album , "Paid In Full". As B's beats backed him up, Rakim's angular monotone shaped caverns and coves of meaning, each line more supportive than exclusive, more evocative than descriptive, more stream-of-consciousness than conscious (Allen, 1987). Yet it wasn't until they released the "remake" of the James Brown mastered, "I Know You Got Soul" by the JB's, did Eric and Ra change the total structure of hip hop. With post-production work by DJ Marly Marl (both "..President" and "...Melody" were remixed by Marly Marl, who was instrumental in helping create the new hip hop standard with his work on their projects) and the "bringing back of old R&B", Eric B and Rakim recognized a musical void of reality that separated rap from true hip hop.

James Brown would loom large in the essence of the hip hop culture. His music became "resurrected" by sampling and looping techniques used by rap and hip hop producers and D.J.'s, who

covertly recognized James Brown as not the God-
father of Soul, but the "Creator of Black Music"[2].
Deep into the latter part of the `80's, "a group of
young men outta Cincinnati, Ohio" (James Brown
protegees') slowly found their previously recorded
movement being sampled into a herd of rap songs.
George Clinton's Parliment-Funkadelic (aka:
PFunk Mob), followed the exact pattern in hip hop
as it did in the Black music transition from Soul to
Funk in the 1970's. Heavy D. and the Boys, Sweet
Tee (with Hurby "Lovebug" Azor's production),
and De La Soul brought the funk music of Parliment
into the foreground of the hip hop movement.
Clinton's genius combination of highly rhythmic,
layered grooves coupled with non-logical and
non-liner lyrics defined what funk was all about
(Vickers, 1984). The keyboard work of Bernie
Worrell, the bass work of Bootsy Collins, the guitar
work of Michael Hampton and Gary Shider, the
voice of Mudbone, and the horn genius of Fred

Wesley, Maceo Parker, and Pee Wee Ellis were acknowledged in various sections of music by a new breed of rap artists who wanted to basically "get funkee".

In 1990, while "the bomb" was still being dropped, jazz began to take shape as the new hip hop directorial dictator. The music of John Coltrane, Sonny Stitt, Miles Davis and other traditional/classic jazz legends found a place in the hip hop musical format. Jazz's rich history (along with the new jazz movement, Spike Lee's "Mo' Better Blues" movie, and the overall original heritage consciousness in the hip hop community) and its' "deja vu" association with hip hop made the relationship almost inevitable. Gang Starr's "Jazz Thang" and Kool G. Rap & DJ Polo's "Streets Of New York" were instrumental in establishing the building of literal hip hop/be bop fusion. Jazz samples were used because they were very similar to the hip hop culture, because it's urban. All the same anger that is said in rap songs is played out on the horn, trumpet or drums. They're the same expression (Premier, 1992). In 1991, A Tribe Called Quest set a new standard in the jazz/rap association by having legendary jazz bassist Ron Carter provide tracks for their "Low End Theory" album. Followed in 1993 by Guru's (of Gang Starr) hip hop/jazz classic collaboration album, "Jazzmatazz", that features Roy Ayers, Donald Byrd, Lionel Hampton just to name a few.

As 1994 approaches rap/hip hop advocates can notice a change, again, in the musical direction of rap. Live bands (Brand New Heavies) and the return of beats (BDP), along with "retronevo" soulful melodic hip hop grooves (Mary J. Blige) have begun to shape the immediate future for rap music. Lyrically the styles will get more intricate, meaningful and graphic, but the musical evolution of hip hop is what needs to be studied in order to determine the direction of rap's elements.

Note II: Again the author failed, but did not forget. This time it's BDP (Sorry Kris). Boogie Down Productions, with Scott La Rock, are solely responsible for creating, redirecting and establishing many, if not all, forms of existing hip hop. Without KRS-One's intellect and vision, the conscious style, the gangsta style, and the reggae would probably not have been accepted by the general hip hop audience, nor the "pseudo" audience who claim the music has no value. It was once said that where KRS-One goes, hip hop goes. True or not, I don't know, but this author definitely will stand behind that statement.

CHAPTER 10

THE GHETTO CODE: Black People's Economic and Social Responsibility In Controlling Rap's Destiny

In Controlling Rap's Destiny

The central problem in the African-american community, outside of economics, is the lack of accountability shared among and for the actions that take place within it. Politically, economically and socially the African-american community is at fault for not supporting itself. We stereotype others, and by our stereotypes we create prisons that keep some in and others out (Asante,1987).   History plays a role in the relationship many Black people have with one another. This has been a long-standing enigma in the movement of Black people living in and against a system.   African-americans have to agree that history is not merely seen as an academic discipline, but , more importantly as a tool by which we conceptualize, plan and validate the correctness and rightness of our ideas and actions, as a people, and as individual members of human community. Understanding our past is essential for race survival and race redemption, and that 1) this is of ever increasing importance in a global society and 2) that our ideas and actions towards race survival and redemption must be judged by the impact they have upon the masses of Black people. The question to ask of ourselves is, given our history and where we are, how does any action and idea serve to further leverage our individual and collective resources towards the higher independence, power and quality of life for the majority of our people (Carruthers, 1984). The African-american is a sort of seventh son, born in veil, and gifted with second-sight in this American world. A world which yields him no true self-consciousness, but only lets him see himself through the revelation of the other world (Du Bois,1903). These factors, along with systematic brainwashing tactics used by the media and school systems, have generations of African-americans mentally lost in comprehending the importance of responsibility in embracing elements of one's culture. Hip hop is a culture that emancipated a culture of being Black, and rap is the verbal culture of that emancipation. Young Black children who were not fortunate enough to have their parents pay for piano lessons, took the music they had and put rhythms over it (Q Tip, 1992). Creating new versions of African communication is essentially what rap music is. Even though a large segment of Africa-America does not agree with this, it is the responsibility of all African-americans to assist in the controlling of this culture's destiny.

Rap music is that action served to "further leverage our individual and collective resources towards the higher independence, power and quality of life for the majority" of Black people. The face of Black revolution and African nationalism has changed from Eldridge Cleaver to Tupac Shakur. From Malcolm X to Aaron (Crunch) Brown. From Angela Davis to Sister Souljah. The sociopolitical movement of the `60's has "bum rushed" the `90's with a microphone, and taken center stage to do the job "politicians" refuse to do. Yet the mindset of a large segment of Africa-Amerikkka refuses to believe this, and detaches itself from the responsibility of supporting the efforts made by rap artists to educate and establish a future for young Black americans living in Amerikkka. All African-americans must realize that they live in a society designed to suppress the importance of... African-americans. Because of this, it is vital that some economic control be placed in the rap arena so that it will remain a product of the community. From a business, self-sufficant and financial standpoint, there is an economically advanced need to foster a system that has more control over record distribution of rap artists. History has proven that entire cultures have been exiled because of a lack of control by the culture-maker, instead of the culture-taker (Jackson,1992). Too often race and racial experiences are used merely as statistical controls rather than as constructs (Matabane,1989). Racism, as it stands in the Black community, is a specific product of capitalism and universal feature of capitalism. Racist and national oppression and discrimination will be completely eliminated only under socialism, national liberation and Black people taking control of products they produce. What is necessary, in this, however hostile environment of capitalism, is a massive, persistent and organized struggle. Whites must realize that Black leadership has come to the fore front in the struggle for Black liberation; and Blacks must realize that Black leadership is essential for any success in this struggle for liberation. This must be a leadership rooted only in the Black community, which alone can pursue the cause of equality without inner contradictions such as those confronting Black capitalists, who are simultaneously victims (like rap artists) of discrimination by white capitalists and exploiters (Perlo,1975).

"We have to be aware of corporate business more than ever. We need to keep an eye on the dollar. It is nothing to do rhymes and tracks, it has to do with your particular business stance and your commitment to the consumer. If in these times there are going top be 20 white rappers coming out in 1996 because it's their (the record companies') business, then what I'm saying is that we got to make it **our** business too. We need to own 15 to 18 of those rappers. We've either gotta buy the record label or buy the group (Ridenhour, 1991). This ideology comes from the mind of a rap artist (Chuck D) who thoroughly has an understanding that the

"freedman" has not yet found in freedom his promised
land (Du Bois, 1903).

The cultural and economic incentive towards
sustaining power in the rap industry has to be passed
along to the masses of African-americans who criticize, denounce, and stigmatize hip hop. Rap music is
a Black youth phenomena that has reached all parts
of the globe. So for African-americans to criticize and
not financially support a medium created by Black
children is basically an upgraded form of suicide. The
lacks who fail to understand the power and significance of the medium seem to be the same ones'
disowning, instead of aiding the Black child. They
should examine the "ghetto code" and realize the
idea of Black youth identifying with their heritage is
very powerful in the feeding of knowledge, and hip
hop is that knowledge-feeder.

CHAPTER 11

A Black To The Future Agenda

Rap simplified is the product of ghetto Darwinism: The survival of the fittest (and the roughest, and the smoothest, and the baddest, and the fastest, and the...). Young African-americans expressing a comprehensive view of contemporary Black America, and attempting to make a profit at the same time. Hip hop, on the other hand, is the movement that enabled rap to find itself, and realize the true potential it had in focusing Black youths lives and values. Giving the Black youth some form of inspiration that informs them about their people, their history, and their culture. Rap artists had the courage and knowledge to lyrically transform their messages, after the profitability was realized.

Researchers have begun to examine systematically how children learn to comprehend and use language through the social learning process. In learning to communicate systematically, children must acquire verbal symbols for objects and events and rules for representing relationships among them (Bandura,1977). What rap is attempting to do with the music is a referencing, so the Black child can understand what is actually a part of them.

The media does not understand this, and it also fails to understand rap. The messages can not be deciphered correctly, so the media exploits the negative image of the culture. White society does not understand rap, and fears that the music can be detrimental to listeners outside of the Black community. Black radio does not support rap, and many African-americans feel that rap is " wrong for singing a song without solutions" (Ridenhour,1990). The fact is that rap music is a part of the African culture. From the first point of the existence of man, music has played a role in communication. The constructive messages, and musical innovation, of rap and hip hop need to be examined as a tool of influence in conditioning social norms among members of the Black community.

Hip hop is over 15 years old, and it is expanding. As it expands, the roots of the younger African-american voice is broadened. This voice is capable of being instrumental in the future direction of the African culture as it exists in America. Hopefully this book will gave some insight to the importance music serves as a vehicle in social learning. The development of today's Black child can be determined by his or her social surroundings. Their points of view can be shaped by what they see and hear. Music plays a role in the life of all those who are exposed to it. African-americans are exposed to rap. The time has come for educators and researchers to recognize rap for what it is : A messenger taking African-america Black to the Future.

CHAPTER 12

On A Mission With No Permission

Treach of Naughty By Nature probably summed up rap's relationship with society by saying, "If you ain't never been to the ghetto, don't come to the ghetto. You wouldn't understand the ghetto. So stay the fk outta the ghetto!". Quietly that may be one of the most important lines in the history of hip hop.

The very bottom line in the hip hop movement is expression. White society (including the media) does not understand "Ghettocentricty", so they are void of truly understanding rap's expression. From this expression has come a new uprise in Black consciousness and Black empowerment. The Black To The Future agenda mentioned earlier has turned into a Black Forever, Backwards Never movement. The elements on paper that Du Bois discussed 90 years ago still haunt today's existing Black society. The problem is that many members of that society do not believe Du Bois' concept applies to them.

Rap music's role in society continues to grow. It has become the focal point of American society. White politicians attack it. The white media degrades it. Wall Street ignores it. MTV exploits it. Corporate America refutes it. Yet it receives the attention that no other single voice in (and from) the Black community receives. For this matter rap music shows more than growth - it shows importance.

Lyrically the activity and diversity found in rap is unmatched by any social or political movement in America (outside of the news). As QTip of A Tribe Called Quest once said, "...people shouldn't denounce rap. They should study it first. Cause (if) you...give a singer four minutes and you give a rapper four minutes, I'll guarantee the rapper will say alot more." In the wake of the 12 year "slavenomics" Ronald Reagan and George Bush have put Black people through, a strong voice, with infectious power, has to be recognized, heard and studied.

Musically rap has fostered a new American child and resurrected a few old ones. Rap has basically followed a pattern of Black music that has already been witnessed. From straight drums (Busy Bee, Cold Crush), to James Brown (P.E., Stetsasonic,Schooly D), to funk (Digital Underground, XClan, Del), to Retronevo Soul (Naughty By Nature, Pete Rock and C.L. Smooth), rap has incorporated these styles of music, and remained the most lyrically innovative form of expression witnessed in the 20th century. The question has to be asked whether the music has caught up with itself? Recreating eras of music at such a fast pace, rap may have exhausted a large majority of it's creativity. The difference in this scenario is economics. Even though many rap artists are <u>not</u> rich, wealthy or millionaires, they are in better economic situations than many of them were in 15 years ago. Because of this (and major record label support was not around back-in-the-day), artists and producers do not have to rely on existing music to be innovative and profitable. The problem will come with acceptability from the hard-core, die-hard rap purist who remembers the roots from which the culture was born. He or she will be the ones who will dictate the future of the music, because they are the ones who will be there, in support, when <u>this</u> cycle repeats itself.

The music has been both the survival and detriment to rap, and its' position in society and the Black community. Any form of music is always considered - entertainment. This paradox is the Catch-44 that enables the "haves" to disregard the voice of the "have-nots", and consider their messages not representative of the people and unworthy of a congressional ear. African people and people of African descent have always been attracted to the rhythmic harmony of a drum beat and The Word. Though-out history we have followed these two catalysts and learned to survive, revitalize and revolutionize generations of people. Rap/Hip Hop is the continuation of an oral-rhythmic tradition that is a part of African heritage. Now we have men and women "on a mission with no permission" to express their concerns, points of views and address issues about Africa-america. Rap has given birth to a generation of young Blacks refusing to let the inbred duality of living in the United States and living "Black" in the United States, make them apathetic.

But the question remains: Is rap the solution? No, but it can be (and right now it is) the driving force behind any collective movement embraced by the Black community. Outside of a few grass-root leaders, and fewer politicians, the Black community has no solidarity on the national-socio-politcal front. The "vibe" that hip hop has created over the past 15-20 years legitimizes it's credibility as a conscious-raising, educational tool for not only the liberation, but the continuance of Black culture in America. It is very important for Black individuals to realize what is written in this book, and understand the ideology being presented on wax (aka:by the rap artists). Mike Mc Gee and Chuck D agree that by 1995, if the Black man and woman don't get "theirs" , then "all hell is going to break lose". Point blank! For Black people to live in this country unemployed AND WITH NO REPARA-

TIONS, is insane. Unless Blacks receive control politically, economically, education-ally, socially, agriculturally, and technically we are going to wake up in the Valley of The Shadow of Death, where all that makes life worth living is marked "For White People Only". Du Bois stated this to be true. Bandura knew this to be true. Rap is informing people that this **will** be true. The time has come for the Black child and the Black community to come together behind and established force "strong" enough to educate and demand change. Or else face the consequences that "hung" us before. 1995 is comin'...Welcome to the Terrordome.

CHAPTER 13

THE EPILOGUE:1996 Dope Fiction or Butter Politics ?

There is a thin line that divides insanity and genius. As a culture, Black people have had to deal with being considered both. For generations African people have made attempts to break the Amerikkkan "spiral of silence" by following social, political, religious, and moral rules established by those "red, white and blue suckas that stole the soul" (Ridenhour, 1990). In a capitalistic society, as America has proven, there is no room for morality. Darwin's theory has become the framework for this country's economic, cultural, and political survival.

Enter rap music. For years the credibility of rap has been tested. Rap has been called everything from the cause of social destruction to the "most brain-dead pop music" ever heard. At the same time rap has open American eyes to Afrocentricity, helped Nelson Mandela survive, and gained the attention of presidential candidates and law enforcement officials. The duality of rap's responsibility to entertain and educate has come full circle. Young Black minds have addressed, created and predicted issues concerning Black American culture, and taken political stands. What was once considered "free-floating rancor" and "tribal acrimony" is now a political network base that is vocally stronger than any combination of Black congressional leaders - and has a larger following. As Chuck D. always says, "Rap is Black America's CNN", but it ain't our Jesse Jackson.

The theory I represent is one of promise, one of fear, and one of solidarity. Considering 1) the powerful following rap music and it's artists have, 2) the concentration and concern the rap culture has for the Black community, and 3) the lack of national political leadership held by African-americans , what would happen if one rap artist ran for President of the United States and promised to appoint other members of the genre in various positions? Think about it. If carefully organized and accurately run, white America could face it's worst nightmare - A real *brotha* holding the title: PRESIDENT.

Black leadership across America is entangled in the thickets of punishing irony: It is riddled by uncertainty precisely when it should be enjoying it's greatest impact in our nation+s history (Dyson,1992). O'Shea Jackson, Carl Ridenhour, Lisa Williamson, Kris Parker, Dana Owens, Aaron

Brown, Tupac Shakur, Lumumba Carson and Jason Hunter, Richard Griffin, and M. Dewese by constitutional rule are eligible for public office. The implementation of these rap artists, along with other members of the Hip Hop nation, into America's political forum will enhance political activity through-out the nation's Black communities. With over 200 Black mayors across the country powerless, one representative in a governors position, no senators, Jesse Jackson failing in two presidential attempts, Lenora Fulani and Ron Daniels not receiving support, Clarence Thomas and Colin Powell blind to Black reality, and an un-collective assembly of Black leaders, the only active alliance continuously evoking verbal concern for the needs of Black individuals worldwide is the

Hip Hop Alliance and certain members of the rap community. They are the only ones who seem to have a general concern for the larger majority of Black Americans, and the only ones willing to take the risks necessary in doing what has to be done to regain "old school" Black Power.

Ice Cube for President! Sound strange? Well let's do this: Establish a politick that has Sister Souljah as Vice President; KRS-One as Secretary of Education; QTip as Secretary of State; Professor Griff as Chief of Staff; Kool Moe Dee, Heavy D., and Doug E. Fresh as drug czars; Queen Latifah, Secretary of Housing & Urban Development; Ice T, Secretary of Defense; XClan and Blackwatch appointed cabinet members; and Chuck D., Commissioner of the FCC. This constituency could control the country, or at least have political control of a large portion of American society.

Systematically, if record sales of each artist were turned into voting potential, this party could receive 125 million votes*. That is about 16 times the amount received by Jesse Jackson, and probably 8 times more than Ross Perot received. The money to run the campaign could come from the artist's personal investments, other members of the rap community (including Russell Simmons, Luke, and Hammer), other Black artists and entrepreneurs (including Spike Lee, Quincy Jones, Eddie Murphy, and Bob Johnson), community, civic and legislative leaders (including Al Sharpton, Mike McGee, Maxine Waters, and Charles Rangle), sports figures (including Jim Brown, Magic Johnson, Deion Sanders, and Craig Hodges), members of the Congressional Black Caucus, the NAACP and other individual contributors. This approach will give this party/ticket independent collective bargaining. The nucleus of Black society will be represented by a cartel of Black people who know the difference between Clarence Thomas and Thurgood Marshall.

Politically Black America is becoming extinct. White America is slowly distancing itself from any affiliation with African-americans in a national political arena. If this trend continues, Blacks in politics in Washington, D.C. will be "harder to find than dinosaur food" (Souljah,1992).

Politics is a numbers game. Reach one, teach some; One man, some votes. Regardless of what ideas a candidate has, or what issues he or she addresses - without votes there is no movement. Rap artists, positive or negative, have the largest following of any collection of Black individuals in America. The time has come to put better use to the African buying dollar and transfer it into "personal priorities of political privledge". Issues concerning the Black community will be at the forefront, and addressed immediately. Think about it: If KRS-One held a national political office would we still beg Congress to implement Afrocentric curriculums in our public school systems? If the Flavor Unit and Digital Underground represented members of the House of Representatives would we have to wait years for an affirmative action or civil rights bill to be passed? If Q Tip was Secretary of State and Shabba Ranks was the Ambassador To The United Nations wouldn't there be human, instead of **inhumane**, treatment of the Haitian refugees? If any serious rap artist were in office, especially those who for years have recorded records about police brutality and treatment of Black civilians, would the Rodney King incident have even occurred? The point being made is there are a great number of Black men and women who collectively have the power to politically move, and make movement for the core of Africa-America. Members of the Hip Hop Nation can be the political organization/group needed to bring total political awareness to young African-americans, dismantle the apathetic nature

of African-americans in general, and elimi-
nate the thought that "if God had wanted us
(Black people) to vote, he would have given
us candidates".

White America's biggest fear has been
either a Black man with a gun, or a Black man
with a following. Today too many Black men
have guns and are doing the wrong things
with them. Any Black leader with a following
who has stood up for the civil rights of his or
her people has been shut down. Amerikkka
has always found a way to put a power limit on
the powerful Black **individual**. At this point,
one individual can not make it happen. Africa-
America needs a force of individuals who
share the same mind-set involving the betterment of Black people nationally and globally.
We need a MOVEMENT, not a move man!
The day of regulating our beliefs and political

power behind <u>one</u> person has to change. It has proven too easy for that person to be stopped. Black America has to face the fact that "the previous move to the white house was the wrong route". Nothing we have done in our history, here in America, has worked. It is time to make an attempt at something new. Something systematic. Something scary.

The Black mainstream has to change; at least in ideology. America's non-compassionate atmosphere has taken it's toll on African-americans. A radical analysis is a solution for a racially-incorrect society. A Hip Hop Alliance/Ice Cube Party may not get the Black man in office, but it will show a "holistic unity" in politics that America has never seen. As a reader, an understanding has to be made that this is a situation that is hypothetical, but is relevant and important to a bigger problem. The rap music industry is strong;

politically in views and financially in money. Yet it remains without power and wealth. Government placement, and lack of political power and leverage have been two of the most devastating areas in the advancement of Black folk. All options have been exhausted, and the future is meaningless. The time has simply come for Africa-America to live up to it's own rhetoric. The madness that surrounds rap has to collectively be turned into the message that comes from rap. Understand? Fear is nothing but a feeling, but actions (successful or unsuccessful) cause change. From a political standpoint, scientists and other political analysts have to realize that any progress toward a significant increase in the national number of a Black elected office will require a coalition of Black candidates with high visibility, notoriety, and the ability to deracialize white peoples' efforts to negate the Black political workforce. Mike McGee, Al Sharpton, Maxine Waters, Mark Ridley-Thomas, Charles Rangle, Don Jackson, Randall Robinson, Louis Farrakhan, Andrew Barrett, Lenord Jeffries, and even Roy Innis have the components to run a national Black political electorate, but they lack the national following, collective political issues, mobilization and visibility to form a political agenda powerful enough to network votes. Rap has the mobilization, collective following, and primary support base necessary to become the force needed in bringing the ideologies of the "unheard" to the front.

White voters are less likely to support those Black politicians who protect what is perceived as a threatening political image (Jones,1991). Yet white society is claimed to be largely responsible for the record-breaking sales of rap music. Where will the white man draw the line between monetary following and political support of those they follow? As rap becomes more important in African-American society, a separation has to be made between attracting a large audience or following, and the dependency on white people. Rap/Hip Hop has been tested and shown that, as an idiom, it can sustain the scrutiny and media racialization placed on all Blacks living in Amerikkka. It has invited the apprehensive and non-apprehensive African-american to "party for your right to fight". It has brought about change, sparked political awareness, and challenged every tactic and activity representative of the American "mainstream". Though inconsistent in certain areas, rap has also been the spokesperson for the larger majority of national and global Black supremacy. Rap has basically filled every qualification needed to represent Black people on a national political base, without being actually qualified. Plus, rap artists realize that in order to truly grasp a hold of America's highest governmental office, death by those who challenge for the position have to be willing to accept death for the position. No other politician seems ready to make that sacrifice.

This is something to think about. Something to cherish. Something to be afraid of. The new movement of Black / Civil Rights power is not going to be the same as the one that moved us 30 years ago. This new group of "statesmen and stateswomen" are fully aware of the mistakes made and the agendas missed during the former movement, and refuse to let that happen again. This new movement will include a political platform. Ice Cube's fictitious run for presidency could be something America has to take seriously. Whether the outcome is victorious or not - credibility will come from this campaign. From this credibility comes power - political power! The same power that got Reagan, as an actor, into the office. Black America needs an established coalition to "wreck shop" on Capitol Hill instead of Pill Hill. Black America needs a group of Black individuals ready and "uniquely qualified" to "handle the whole weight" Africa-America has to carry. Black America needs Chuck D in charge of the Federal Communications Commission to correct these ill-placed, distorted messages and images about African-americans that come from television and advertising. Black America needs KRS-One to head the nation's education department so that a "brotha" who has always treated us right can teach us right. Black America needs XClan as cabinet members in the House of Representatives to give "our house" strong and true representatives. **Black America needs Ice Cube for President and Sister Souljah for Vice President.**

A progressive Black political agenda is what is at stake. Advocating housing and health programs, affirmative action, Afrocentric and multicultural education, income and jobs for those unemployed, African foreign trade and total divestment from South Africa are only parts of the platform unaddressed by American government as it relates to African-americans. This we have to stop! The next revolution should be more than televised - it should be political. Political to the point where whites lose control, Malcolm X has a national holiday, South Africa-America no longer exists, and every rap album sold is equal to a Black vote made. Think about it...

REFERENCES

Dyson, Michael Eric. "Grass Roots Leaders".

Emerge, May 1992. p. 31.

Jones, Charles. 1991. "Blacks & American Politics". Western Journal of Black Studies.
    Vol. 15, No.2. pp.105 - 113

Ridenhour, Carlton. Lyrics from "Who Stole The

Soul". 1990.

Souljah, Sister. Lyrics from "360 Degrees of

Power". 1992.

* estimated record sales of rap music by the end of 1992.
    Source: Billboard 1991

REFERENCES

Bandura, A., (1977). Social Learning Theory. New Jersey:Prentice-Hall.

Blackwell, J., (1975). "The Black Community: Diversuty and Unity." The Black Scholar, 7.

Bolden, D., (1989,Oct.). "Youths Communicate Through Rap". The Final Call. p.19.

Chesboro, J.W., Foulger, D.A., Nachman, J.E., & Yanilli, A., (1985). "Popular Music As A Mode of Communication, 1955-1982". Critical Studies In Mass Communication, 2.

Du Bois, W.E.B. (1903). The Souls Of Black Folks. New York: New American Library.

Ellul, J., (1969). Propaganda: The Foundation Of Men's Attitudes. New York: Knopf.

Gandy, O., (1982). Beyond Agenda Setting: Information Susidies and Public Policy. New Jersey: Ablex.

George, N., (1989). The Death Of Rhythm & Blues. New York: Patheon.

Graber, D., (1984). Mass Media and American Politics. 2nd ed.,Washington, DC. Congressional Quarterly Inc.

Gunderson, E., (1990, March). "Listen Up" . USA Today, p.4D.

Hicks, P.T., (1987). The Relationship Between An Oral Rhythmic Style of Communication (rap music) and Learning Retention In The Urban Pre-School. (Master's Thesis, Howard University, 1987).

Hunter, J., (1990). X Clan [Press Release]. New York: 4th & Broadway Records.

Jackson, Jesse. Interviewed by MTV, July 1989.

Johnson, R., (1989). Expanding The Black Voice In Telecommunications. Presented at the One-Third Of A Nation Conference, Howard University.

Kofsky, F., (1970). Black Nationalism and The Revolution In Music. New York: Pathfinder.

Lang, G.E., and Lang, K., (1981). Watergate: An Exploration Of Agenda Setting Process. In G.C. Wilhoit & H. Debock (eds.) Mass Communication Review Year Book, 2, p. 447-

68.

Kot, G., (1990, April). "Raps Bad Rap" The Chicago Tribune. Sec.B, p.4.

Lasswell, H., (1948). "The Structure and Function Of Communication n Society". The Communication Of Ideas, ed. L.Bryson. New York: Harper.

Lippman, W., (1922).Public Opinion. New York: Harcort.

Lull, J., (1985). "On The Communicative Properties Of Music". Communication Reseach, 12, p. 363-372.

MacConkey, D. I., (1974). Teens and The Mass Media: A Study OBlack and White Adolescents and Their Use Of The Mass Media. (Doctorial Dissertation, University of Maryland, 1974).

Merriam, A.P., (1964). The Anthropology Of Music. Evanston: University of Illinois.

Needs, C., (1989, June)."Rap : The Breakdown". Dance Music Report, p. 4-60.

Needs, C., (1989, July). "Stupid Def". Dance Music Report, p. 58-84.

Reich, H., (1990, Aug.). "Bird Spoke A Language Of Jazz That GivesVoice To His Genius". The Chicago Tribune, p. 16.

Ridenhour, Carlton. Interviewed by Spin Magazine, July, 1988.

Waltrous, P., (1990, March). "Raps Trip To A New and Surreal   Territory". New York Times.

Winthrope, O., (1988). "Taking It To The Streets: Rap In America".   Music Express, p. 35.

FOOTNOTES

1. Max Roach, interviwed by Frank Owen, Octo ber 1988.
2. Newsweek, "Rap Rage". March, 1990. pp.56-63.
3. Chuck D., interviewed by author, April 1990.
4. Compiled from Billboard Magazine's 1990 Year End Issue,   Dec/Jan. 1990.
5. Ice T., interviewed by Alan Light, Roling Stone, August 1992.

extra:
Shomari, H. (1992) On Cultural Revolution: KRS-One and The Struggle To Democratize Mass Media. Presented at The 3rd Annual Conference On Countering Global White Supremacy. The Center For Inner City Studies.
(unpublished).

Hip Hop has changed since it was first introduced to America over 15 years ago. Careers have been made and lives have been lost, but the true essence of the hip hop culture has remained in tact and in the hands of those who understand it's importance. Robert "Scoop" Jackson is one of those individuals. This "music historian" has taken the world of literature by storm. Through countless numbers of articles that have appeared in national magazines and newspapers, and as editor of the ground-breaking magazine, The Agenda, Mr. Jackson has raised the consciousness-level of African-American readers by providing them with direct insight into the world of young Black America and hip hop. This book, *The Last Black Mecca: Hip Hop*, is the first true in-depth look at the total effect hip hop and rap have had on the African-American community. Economics, politics, radio and the media all have played roles in shaping what has now being called "the second coming of jazz". Mr. Jackson addresses these issues, and takes a critical stance on what the future holds for the music, the culture and the society that embraces it.

Look for the follow-up, *Profits of Rage* to appear in the near future. This is only the beginning.

The WORLD of
AFRICAN

$20.00

MUSIC

Written
and
edited
by
Ronnie
Graham

**Stern's Guide
to
Contemporary
African Music**

PLUTO

VOLUME TWO

Following the huge success of **Stern's Guide to Contemporary African Music** Volume 1, first published by Pluto in 1988, this entirely new book brings the story up to date.

This second volume, **The World of African Music**, is a sequel as well as a companion volume that reflects recent developments in the market: the huge growth in the industry — at least 4,000 new recordings were released between 1988 and 1991 — and the new stars and styles that have emerged.

Black Sisters, Speak Out

Black Women and Oppression in Black Africa

By Awa Thiam **$12.95**

Women are the last great colony in the world, and the Muslim women of Black Africa the most colonized of all. Poligamy, clitoridectomy and sewing up the vagina (infibulation) are the weapons used by men to control women.In this powerful and moving book, **AWA THIAM**, a Black African woman, lets oppressed women in the world speak for themselves. She makes plain that these practices are not remote and 'barbaric', but part of a pattern of universal violence displayed by the oppressive system.

African Origins of Major World Religions $13.95

The papers contained in this issue represent the proceedings from the Afrikan Origins of Civilization Conference of 1986. The theme is the importance of the African in the birth and influence of the major world religions.

By Yosef Ben-Jochannan, Charles Finch, Tsegaye Gabre-Medhin, Modupe Oduyoye

Ancient Egypt and Black Africa
$13.95 *by T.Obenga*

This collection represents the texts of four lectures delivered by the author at the School of Oriental & African Studies. The essays deal with Ancient Egyptian philosophy, influences of the former on the formation of Greek philosophy and science, comparative African, Ancient Egyptian, Sematic and G r e c o - L a t i n linguistics, and the first attempt by the author to deal with the presence and regognition of women in Ancient Egyptian life.